When an angel calls.

by

Colin Boynton

COPYRIGHT:
COLIN
BOYNTON 2017

ISBN: 978-0-9559931-7-6

WHEN AN ANGEL CALLS.

When an angel calls your name
There's nothing you can do,
But give yourself up gracefully
Be silent and be true.

You know you cannot fight them,
You cannot hide away,
They'll come and get you anytime,
Any night or day.

PART 1 - BEGINNINGS.

Together they lived peacefully
Year, by year, by year.
They had their quarrels, had their fights,
But still their love held dear.

Enjoyed each others company,
Made the best of life,
Doing things together,
A husband and a wife.
They'd met up many years ago
Just after starting school,
Spent many happy days together
Breaking every rule.

They wished to be together,
Didn't want to part,
Decided to get married,
From the very start.
Courting days were happy,
And courting days were fun,
Spent huddled under raindrops
Or sat out in the sun.

They'd wander in the country,
Or wander on the beach,
He gave her all she wanted
With nothing out of reach.
He promised moon, he promised stars,
And love forever more,

They'd be together
two as one,
While sitting on the
shore.
Watching stars up in
the sky
The waves upon the
sand,
Raindrops gently
falling down
Sitting hand in hand.
With picnics in the
country

A stroll down country lanes,
Who could wish for any more
As the moonlight wanes.
Starting out together
The future looking bright,
The hardships and the heartaches,
Were hidden out of sight.

It didn't seem to matter
What life might have in store,
They'd always have each other,
Who could wish for more?
Yet people tried to part them,
Told them it was wrong,

They shouldn't stay together
No way did they belong.
She was very gentle
Sheltered as a child,
He was very rugged
Often running wild.
She would sit home reading
Or learning how to bake,

He would be out
playing sports
Or swimming in the
lake.
She was very quiet
Always went to
church,
He was loud and
noisy
Always on the search.
For just one more
adventure,
One more thing to do

She was quite content to watch
Their love just grew and grew.
Something seemed to draw them,
Brought them ever close,
They'd fell in love at first sight,
That's how the story goes.

And every day they walked to school
Together hands held tight,
Sharing all the jokes and laughs
Returning home at night.
Nothing ever changed them
Each day stayed the same,

Through the rain or sunshine,
This wasn't just a game.
They knew from the beginning
There'd be no other love,
True to one another
Blessed from up above.
Eyes for one another,

Each minute spent apart,
Only made love stronger
Deep within the heart,
Two children who were so in love
Who thought that it could last,
Their parents always thought,
Their love could not hold fast.

Too young for them to fall in love,
Too young is what they said,
Too young to be together,
Too young for them to wed.
They told them they should wait a while
Or they might just regret,

A choice made while they both were young
They told them to forget.
No matter what their friends all said
Or how their parents tried,
They'd made their minds up long ago
Their love they could not hide.

Two people who were so in love
Could not be torn apart,
For if it ever happened,
Would break each others heart.

PART 2 - A START AND END.

The early days of marriage
Were spent in joyful fun,
Doing things together,
A new life just begun.
Planning for the future,
Deciding what to do,

Where to spend their life as one
So many things now new.
Should they start a family?
Or should they simply wait?
Buy a house together
Before it was too late?
Did they want to travel

And go around the world,
Taking opportunities
Being brave and bold.
It didn't take them very long
To settle on their choice,
With good intentions starting out
They had two little boys.
Two tiny little babies,

Bundles made of joy,
Sleepless nights with worry
They looked just like a toy.
One seemed bright and very strong
The other quiet and small,
One was eating all the time
The other not at all.

And then one Monday morning
Early in the day,
She felt that something wasn't right,
She knew it straight away.
Running to the bedroom
To find them lying there,

One was sleeping peacefully
Without a simple care.
The other didn't move at all
His eyes were closed quite tight,
Her tiny little baby boy
Had passed away that night.

She held him gently in her arms
The tears began to fall,
Trying hard to understand
The meaning of it all.
Why should one so young as this
Be taken from her care,
And all alone inside the house

Her husband wasn't there.
He'd gone to work that morning,
Cheerfully he'd gone,
Unaware of what would come
Before the day was done.
The call came through that morning
He had to get back home,

He heard his wife was crying
While he was on the phone.
No clues to what had happened
Of what was going on,
He made his way back quickly
In the morning sun.
His wife was waiting for him

She held him very tight,
As she broke the news to him
About their loss that night.
They shed their tears together,
And shared the grief as one,
Gaining strength together

Although it felt quite wrong.
They knew they had to say goodbye
And had to let him go,
On the day they buried him
In the winter snow.
Although the day was freezing
They never felt the cold,

Just a numbness in
their hearts
And one of feeling
old.
Their tears were born
in sorrow,
Their heartache born
in grief,
They knew they never
would forget
Or ever get relief.
They held their other
little boy

To keep him safe and warm,
And wandered slowly from the grave
Serene and very calm.
People vanished slowly,
Soon they were alone,
The two of them and one small boy
The other boy now gone.

Gone but not forgotten,
He'd stay a memory,
With them through their lifetime
To keep them company.

PART 3 – FAMILY LIFE.

Their little boy was four years old
Their world was in a whirl,
The news that they were given was -
"It's a little girl!"
All that they had hoped for,

A dream had now come true,
A complete little family
Now dressed in pink and blue.
Those tears of those few years ago
The sorrow they had had,
This little girl soon took away

Those feelings that were sad.
They went for picnics in the park
They always fed the ducks,
They took along some balls and games
And sometimes picture books.
Life was now quite happy,

And life for them complete
The four of them a family
Strolling down the street.
Sometimes they went down to the beach
To play down by the sea,
Other days were spent in town
Happy and carefree.

The days of school upon them
Left the house quite still,
Until each evening they returned
Running up the hill.
Laughter ringing from them
Loud and very clear,
Getting so much louder

When they were very near.
The joy within that family
Was very clear to see,
Two very happy children
Running home for tea.
Games were played together,
Stories told at bed,
Pain was healed with kisses

And soft words that were said.
Meal times spent together
With lots to talk about,
What they'd done at school that day
Or what they'd seen when out.
On sunny summer evenings

They'd go out for a walk,
Picking lot's of flowers
Laugh and sing and talk.
And when the winter winds
Were cold when they did blow,
They'd wait with anxious faces
Ready for the snow.

Making snowmen in the field,
Or sliding on the ice,
Getting cold and very wet
It still was very nice.
Nothing seemed to matter
They just had lots of fun,
When the snow had fallen
And in the winter sun.

Arriving home together
This family of four,
Would leave their coats and wellies
Beside the old back door.
Then run inside to warm up,
Standing by the fire,
And one by one they'd have a bath

And then they would retire.
And when they lay down quietly
With bedtime stories read,
The children very sleepy
Were tucked up tight in bed.
Two very happy children

Were very soon asleep,
Tired from the days events
With memories to keep.
Back downstairs content and quiet
Two people felt at ease,
After all the daytime noise

They had a little
peace.
Sipping on a cup of
tea
Down by the fireside,
Chatting with each
other
Until they too retired.

PART 4 – MOVING OUT – MOVING ON

The years passed by so quickly,
The children soon left home,
Once they both had finished school
They left them all alone.

They started families
of their own
And soon moved far
away,
One went to Australia
And one went New
York way.
It gave them chance
to travel
See far off distant
lands,
To visit both the
families

Explore exotic sands.
Returning home to England
Was still a treasured thing,
Returning to their home life
And all that it could bring.
The years passed by quite quickly,
But both remained content,

They liked the life
routine they had
And how their time
was spent.
Summers in the
garden,
Winters warm inside,
Reminding them of
years ago
When they were
groom and bride.
They now did things
they wanted

The two of them alone,
No need to think of others
With the family gone.
Life became more simple,
Work soon passed them by,
And after years of toiling hard
Came time to say goodbye.

No tears of sorrow
was there,
A new life could now
start,
A time to be together
Instead of being apart.
They settled down so
very fast,
To their new found
life,
They started doing
many things

As husband and his wife.
Days out in the country,
Walking down a lane,
Sitting by the seaside
Things they did again.
Life was very pleasant
And happy for them too,
And life was very busy

With lots of things to do.
Romance blossomed once again
Their love was ever strong,
The two were never parted
Could anything go wrong?
They both seemed very happy
Ill health kept away,

So they lived their lives full up
Day by day by day.
All the things they never did,
And always wanted to,
Were things they now were doing
And time so quickly flew.
And as the years soon quickly passed

Their age began to show,
They couldn't do the same things now
They had to go more slow
But still they loved each other,
As anyone could see,
Then one day when out with friends
He dropped down on one knee.

"We did it years ago my dear
Let's do it one more time.
Will you marry me my love
Will you just be mine?"
50 years together,
Their vows renewed with love,
A marriage made in heaven

And blessed from up above.

PART 5 - LOOKING BACK

They married in the early spring
The sun was shining bright,
Showing off her beauty
All dressed up in white.
They'd made a life together

Building up a home,
Working hard through every day
The weekends spent alone.
They often went out walking,
With days spent by the sea,
Enjoying time together
And soon they became three.

They'd shared the joy and laughter
And wiped away the tears,
As their children grew up
Through the happy years.
Through schooldays with their worries
The children hadthen left home,

Leaving just the two of them
Once again alone.
They'd soon picked up the pieces
Of how things used to be,
Now sitting in the countryside
Or sitting by the sea.
They'd been away at weekends,

And visited old friends,
Went on foreign holidays
To far off distant lands.
Those things they'd never tried to do
With a family,
Now they made up for those times
Happy to be free.

Here there was two people
So happy as a pair,
Spending time together
And everything they'd share.
The tears and all the laughter,
The heartache and the pain,
Times so filled with sunshine

And stormy days with rain.
It didn't seem to matter
What life would throw their way,
They always had each other
There both night and day.
And then one day she noticed

Something not quite right,
The man that she called husband
Had been awake all night.
The pain had come on slowly,
They knew that it was wrong,
The doctors diagnosis said

His days were almost done.
They shed a gentle tear or two,
And held each other tight,
She promised she would be with him
Through each day and night.
The days passed very quickly,

Time was running out,
Each day he said "I Love You
Of that I have no doubt"
Each night she kissed her husband
And said a little prayer,
Not knowing if the morning

Would find him lying there.
That night he kissed her gently,
And held her hand so tight,
The tears rolled gently down her cheeks
She never left his sight.
As the clock chimed midnight

He turned his head and smiled,
He said "I love you sweetheart"
His voice just like a child.
He gently lay back on the bed,
And closed his eyes again,
The last breath left his body

No longer filled with pain.

PART 6 - FORGET AND BE FREE.

She wandered through the countryside
Alone, yet unafraid,
No knowing where she's going
Or the choices she has made,
Alone she wandered by the trees

Then sat amongst the flowers,
Watching clouds drift slowly by
Counting out the hours.
It now seemed quite impossible
To think of what she'd done,
The memory might haunt her

Her life spent on the run.
In her mind she wandered
Through meadows bright and gay,
Not knowing where she's going
But going every day,
The freedom that she felt there
Out among the flowers,

Nothing there could harm her
She wandered there for hours.
It now felt quite impossible
She'd done what she had done,
Would anybody find out
Would anybody come?

Through the fields she wandered
Happy to be free,
Then hiding in the long grass
So no one else could see,
It seemed like many years now
Since she'd had the chance
To wander in a meadow

To walk, to skip, to dance.
It still seemed quite impossible
To think what she had done
And no one tried to stop her
She just kept moving on.
Each minute that she wandered

And every step she took,
She left behind the life she knew
Without a second look,
She never gave a second thought
Just glad that she was free,
To wander in the countryside

Alive and quite carefree.
It now seems quite impossible
At all that she had done
That no one even missed her
Had noticed she had gone.
Although she had a family

And still had many friends,
Most of them just visited
On the odd weekends,
And no one noticed that she'd gone
They never saw her go
She wandered out at night time
Her step was soft and slow.

It should have been impossible
To do what she had done
But there she was that morning
Sitting in the sun.
She didn't have the memories
She didn't have a care
The illness that she suffered
Left her unaware,

Of any kind of danger
And how things just might be
The illness robbed her of her life
She really did not see.
It really seems impossible
She'd done what she had done
Looking back on everything

Now the time had come.
That evening as she lay down
A pillow made of grass
She looked up in the night sky
And watched the evening stars,
The cold crept slowly on her
She never felt it come

She closed her eyes to fall asleep
But now her life was done.
It really felt impossible
She'd done what she had done,
And when they found her lying there
They found her life had gone.

Lying in the morning mist
A smile still on her face
Who knew what she'd been smiling at
Lying in that place,

Did anybody worry?
Or anybody care?
Did that lonely lady
Die with no one
there?

When an angel calls
your name
There's nothing you
can do
And sometimes when
they call a name
There's someone else
there too!

Copyright :
COLIN BOYNTON
2017

www.ingramcontent.com/pod-product-compliance
Lightning Source LLC
Chambersburg PA
CBHW071318040426
42444CB00009B/2044